Lauro De Bosis
Story of My Death

Translated by Ruth Draper

ERIS
gems

TOMORROW AT 3 O'CLOCK IN A meadow on the Cote d'Azur, I have an appointment with Pegasus.

Pegasus is the name of my airplane. It has a russet body and white wings. It is as strong as eighty horses and as slender as a swallow. It gorges on gasoline and leaps through the sky like its brother of old; but at night, it can glide at will through the air like a phantom. I found it in the Hercynian forest and its old master is going to bring it to me on the shores of the Tyrrhenian Sea, believing in perfect sincerity that it will serve the idle pleasures of a young Englishman. My bad accent has not awakened his suspicions. I hope he will pardon my ruse!

And yet we are not going to chase chimeras, but bring a message of liberty to a people in chains across the seas. To drop my imagery (which was needed so as to leave discreetly vague the origins of my airplane), we are going to Rome to scatter these words of liberty far and wide, words which for seven years have been forbidden like a crime. And with reason, for if they had been allowed, they would have shaken the fascist tyranny to its foundations within a few hours.

Every regime in the world, even the Afghan and the Turkish, allows its subjects some liberty. Fascism alone, in self-defense, must annihilate all thought. It cannot be blamed for punishing more severely than patricide any belief in liberty and any sign of loyalty to the Constitution, for that is the only way it can survive. It cannot be blamed for deporting thousands of citizens without trial or for dealing out 7,000 years of imprisonment in the space of four years. How could it dominate a free people if it did not terrorize them with its black garrison of 300,000 hitmen?

Fascism has no choice. If one shares its point of view, one is obliged to agree with its apostle, Mussolini, when he says that "Liberty is a putrefied corpse." If one wishes fascism to last, one must approve the murder of Matteotti, the rewards meted out

4

to his murderers, the abolition of freedom of the press in Italy, the sacking of Croce's house, the millions spent on espionage and on agents provocateurs; in short, the sword of Damocles suspended over the head of every citizen.

The Austrians in 1850, the Bourbons and the other tyrants of Italy never went this far. They never deported people without trial by law. The total number of sentences passed by their tribunals never reached the figure of 7,000 years' imprisonment in four years. Above all, they never enrolled the very sons of their victims in their army of hitmen. Fascism does this. It snatches children from the age of eight from every family (even if they are Liberal or Socialist), makes them wear the uniform of executioners and gives them a barbaric and warrior education. "Love the rifle, worship the machine gun and do not forget the dagger." Thus wrote Mussolini in an article for children.

You cannot both admire fascism and deplore its excesses. Its existence is dependent on its excesses. Its excesses are its logic. The logic of fascism is to exalt the hitman and slap Toscanini in the face. It has been said that the murder of Matteotti was a mistake: from the fascist point of view, it was a stroke of genius. Fascism has been criticized for torturing its prisoners in order to extort confessions from them. But if it wants to survive it cannot do otherwise.

The foreign press should understand this. There is no prospect of fascism becoming merciful and human without its ceasing to exist. Fascism has grasped the situation and for seven years Italy has been turned into a great prison, where children are taught to cherish the chains that bind them and to pity those who are unbound. Twenty-year-old youth cannot remember any other atmosphere. The name of Matteotti is almost unknown to them. Since the age of thirteen they have been told that men have no rights except those that the State decides to grant them according to its whims. Many believe this. The myth that Mussolini saved

Italy from Bolshevism is accepted with no discussion.

But do not think that Italy is duped into believing this. The proof that the great majority of Italians is profoundly antifascist is provided by the regime itself with its fear of any whispering and with the ferocity with which it punishes even the smallest expressions of freedom of thought. A regime that is sure of its own strength never needs to take refuge in such measures.

In June 1930, I began to issue a bimonthly letter, strictly constitutional in character, in which I explained the need for an agreement among all men of law and order in view of the day in which fascism will fall. Since fascism seems to have adopted the motto "after me the deluge", the initiative was most opportune; and, in fact, the letters, using the chain-letter system, began to circulate by the thousands. For five months, I was able to carry out this work completely on my own. Every fortnight, I would mail 600 letters signed "National Alliance" asking that each recipient make six copies and send them to six addresses.

Unfortunately, in December, during a short trip abroad which I had to undertake, the police arrested the two friends who had agreed to assume the task during my absence. They were tortured and sentenced to fifteen years in prison. One of them, Mario Vinciguerra, one of the best Italian authors, a literary and art critic, despite being ill, was left all night (a night in December) on the terrace of the police headquarters. Then, they hit him repeatedly so hard that he completely lost his hearing in one ear. They threw him in a cell six feet square with not even a chair to sit on and every morning his bed would be removed. Following the protests of foreign governments and of eminent English and American political figures, their conditions were improved. Mussolini even went so far as to offer them their liberty on condition that they would sign a letter of submission to the regime. They both refused.

The day I read that my friends had been arrested, I was about to cross the border to return to Italy. Naturally, my first impulse was to go back to Rome and share their fate, but I realized that the duty of a soldier is not to surrender to the enemy but to fight until the end. So, I immediately decided to go to Rome, not to surrender, but to carry on the work of the National Alliance by throwing four hundred thousand letters; then, either fall in combat or return to my base to prepare other raids.

The sky of Rome has never been violated by enemy planes; I shall be the first, I said to myself; and I started preparing for the enterprise right away.

It was not easy, because for a poet it is always difficult to earn a living, and if he is in exile during a year of economic crisis, we should not be surprised if he descends very fast the steps of Bohemian life.

I was hired as a concierge at the Hotel Victor Emmanuel III, on the Rue de Ponthieu, in Paris. My republican friends said that I was punished where I had sinned! To tell the truth, I was not only concierge but also manager and telephone operator. Sometimes, three or four bells would ring at the same time and I would scream in the stairwell, at the top of my lungs: "Irma, a double butter to number 35!" As preparation for my raid on Rome it wasn't much. However, in between the baker's bill and receipts to customers, I wrote a message to the King of Italy and studied the map of the Tyrrhenian Sea.

The rest of my preparations is the most interesting part of the story but unfortunately it must remain a secret. In May, I carried out my first flight alone in a Farman plane, around Versailles. Then, having learned that my secret had reached the ears of the Fascists, I disappeared and reappeared in England with a different name. On July 13, I left Cannes in an English plane carrying eighty kilos [175 lbs.] of leaflets. Since I only had five hours of flight to my credit, I went by myself so as not to risk the life of a friend.

Unfortunately, an accident interrupted my enterprise on the coast of Corsica and I had to leave the plane in a field. My secret had been unveiled. In Italy, they had no problem understanding who the mysterious pilot was. The police of England and France started a search with an eagerness that flattered me. They even argued about who was to have my portrait. I am sorry for the inconvenience I have caused them.

The worst part was that now I could no longer count on the surprise factor, my biggest chance for success. Nonetheless, Rome became for me what Cape Horn was to the Flying Dutchman; dead or alive, I vowed to get there. My death (while annoying for me because I have so many things to accomplish) could only increase the success of my flight. Since the dangers are all in the return flight, death could only come after I deliver my 400,000 letters, which will therefore come with an even stronger recommendation!

After all, it is a way to display a small example of civic spirit and to attract the attention of my fellow citizens to the irregularity of their situation. I am convinced that fascism will not end unless some twenty youths sacrifice their lives to shake the spirit of Italians. While during the Risorgimento there were youths by the thousands ready to give their lives, today, there are very few. Why? It is not because the courage of today's youth is inferior to that of their fathers. It is that no one takes Fascism seriously. Everyone, including its chiefs, believes that its end is imminent, so it would be out of proportion to give one's life for something that will crumble on its own. This is a mistake. It is necessary to die. I hope that others will follow and will succeed in shaking public opinion.

The only thing I need to do now is give the text of my three messages.

The first one is directed to the King. I tried to interpret the sentiment of the mass of my people by abstracting from their sentiments. I think that a republican as well as a monarchist could support it. We just pose the dilemma: For liberty or against it? His grandfather, after the most terrible defeat in Italian history, resisted the Austrian Marshal who wanted to force him to repeal the Constitution. Does he, after the greatest victory in Italian history (the victory of the Liberals), really want to let the last strip of Constitution die without moving a finger?

In addition to my letters, I will throw several copies of a magnificent book by Bolton King, *Fascism in Italy*. As you throw bread on a starving city, on Rome you need to throw history books.

After flying at a height of 12,000 feet over Corsica and the Island of Montecristo, I will arrive over Rome around 8 pm, having flown the last twenty kilometers with engines off. While I have had only seven and a half hours of flight training, if I fall it will not be for pilot error. My plane only flies 150 km an hour, whereas Mussolini's fly at 300 km/hr. He has 900 planes and they all received the order to machine gun down, at any cost, any suspect plane.

No matter how little they know me, they must realize that, after my first attempt, I have not given up. If my friend Balbo (who is called Italy's greatest "thief") has done his duty, they are now waiting for me. So much the better. I will be worth more dead than alive.

L.d.B.

ERIS

An imprint of Urtext
Unit 3 2 Dixon Butler Mews
London, W9 2BU

Printed in Great Britain

The moral rights of the author and translator
have been asserted.

ISBN 978-1-912475-87-2

eris.press